THE COMING ORDER

THE COMING ORDER

Reflections on Sovietology and the Media

Andrei Navrozov

The Claridge Press
London

All rights reserved. No part of this publication may be reproduced or transmitted in any form or by any means, including photocopying and recording, without the written permission of the copyright holder, application for which should be addressed to the publishers. Such written permission must also be obtained before any part of this publication is stored in a retrieval system of any nature.

First published in Great Britain 1991

by The Claridge Press
6 Linden Gardens
London W2 4ES
and Box 420
Lexington
Georgia 30648

Copyright © Andrei Navrozov

Printed by
Short Run Press
Exeter, Devon

ISBN 1-870626-03-6

Navrozov, Andrei: *The Coming Order: Reflections on Sovietology and the Media*

1. Politics

Introduction

It was once explained to a Southern legislator in Congress that Eisenhower was not a *communist* but an *anti-communist*. 'Well', drawled the southerner in reply, 'I don't care what kind of communist he is'.

I recalled this anecdote while reviewing a book by Walter Laqueur, one of the intellectual coryphaei of Western 'anti-communism'. The founder and first editor of *Survey*, since 1955 a leading journal in the field of Soviet studies, chairman of the International Research Council of the Center for Strategic and International Studies in Washington, author of fifteen books on Soviet and international affairs, Professor Laqueur described his latest topical endeavour on the acknowledgements page as 'work on de-Stalinization and the debates on Stalinism', receiving sponsorship from no less prominent a Conservative than Conrad Black, owner of the Telegraph empire.

The anecdote involving the southern gentleman came to mind because, looking back on the history of Western response to the Soviet regime's evolutionary development, I can think of no political aphorism that better captures the ordinary man's disdain for ideology as the great befuddler of common sense, nor his natural understanding that this, indeed, is its sole intended function. In the twentieth century, behaviour, such as criminal activity on a mass scale, is not motivated by ideologies: ideologies, such as militant nationalism, exist to justify behaviour.[1] Totalitarian suppression of liberty, for instance, is undertaken because it maximizes the power of an oligarchy, not because the undertaking is inherently 'Marxist' or 'National Socialist', 'Communist' or 'Fascist'.

If we believe that the ordinary man is not an abstraction, we must concede that people like Professor Laqueur are ultimately his teachers. They write newspaper leaders and advise politicians, frame educational and taxation policies, appear on television to pronounce on international affairs, chair committees, staff think-tanks and issue warnings on national security or the environment. Tenured academics or freelance intellectuals, they shape his world view, affect his beliefs and opinions, influence his conduct. Yet people like Professor Laqueur have over the years proven to be worse teachers than those they proposed to teach. The ordinary man still has the will to resist being befuddled. His teachers lost it long ago, or else they became so numerous that common sense fell victim to the statistical average.

It is with sampling that statistical average that I am concerned here. The scope of this essay will be limited to the response of a segment of the British press to the current reform of the Soviet power structure and to the emergence, against a background of a 'new openness' in Russia, of the most viable form of totalitarianism as well as the most cunning and ruthless dictator since Stalin's day. Were I writing for an American audience, my task would have been made more concrete by the unchallenged monopoly exercised by a single newspaper, *The New York Times,* in the field of serious journalism and hence its overwhelming preponderance in every political context including this one.[2] By contrast, in Europe and especially in Britain the press remains diverse, even feudally so, not only at the mass level where competitive tabloids battle for market share, but also at the level of quality journalism where standard-bearers of media empires compete for influence and prestige. As the reader shall see, I focus on *The Times* in my search for the common denominator of opinion not because it is as suffocatingly influential as its New York namesake but because of its specific position in the mainstream of British politics.

The First Circle

That a military power is only as successful with respect to equipotent adversaries as its strategic deception of those adversaries was axiomatic for Sun Tzu, a Chinese general writing centuries before the birth of Christ. In our own era, however, with its unprecedented concentration of scientific and technological knowledge in the nations of Western Europe, deception lost much of its pre-eminence in strategic thinking as the essentially homogenous Christian states evolved into what we know today as Western democracies. It is only with the advent of totalitarianism in 1917, when 'Western' science and technology fell into the hands of a fundamentally heterogenous adversary, that strategic deception can once again be said to have become the backbone of global *Realpolitik*, leaving conventional diplomacy to Western diplomats. It is interesting to note that even the Russian-born editor of the English translation of Clausewitz's *On War*[3] does not mention 'strategic deception' anywhere in the book's exhaustive conceptual index: quite simply, in 1832, such a concept would have been subsumed under a variety of diplomatic rubrics.

During the past seventy-three years, for historical reasons too numerous to list here even in brief, the West has had no unified geopolitical strategy in its effort to defeat, or at least contain, its new and altogether novel adversary. That is why my present quest of an intellectual common denominator is so timely. From 1917 to 1963, the West enjoyed total strategic superiority over its totalitarian adversary by virtue of its historic 'head start' in science and technology, whereupon that superiority began to wane. Hence what was said or done about the Soviet threat between 1917 and 1963 is now of less consequence than what has been said or done about it since then, and especially during the last decade.

What strategies have existed in the West can be said to have been misdirected against the adopted ideology of totalitarianism, a mere component of an evolving deception. No sooner did the West's strategists defeat their adversary's ideological 'argument' with the triumphalism of medieval disputants than it was revised, dropped or substituted by another set of equally arbitrary contentions. Their adversary's gains, meanwhile, were only too real.

Thus seventy-three years later, for reasons equally numerous and complex, it is nearly impossible to invoke the fundamental principle of totalitarianism's strategy in polite discourse in the West without being diagnosed as a paranoiac. Indeed, since the diagnosis is psychologically defensive, one may well infer that what one's interlocutors fear most is fear itself. In my own experience, the thinker most often used by my interlocutors as a scapegoat in recent years has been my compatriot Anatoly Golitsyn. I need not dwell on the infamous defector's career in the West, and for the purposes of this discussion I accept the common, though quite possibly simplistic, view of his main premise, namely, that *all* information originating within a totalitarian state is deception.

Golitsyn qualified for scapegoat status when he went on record maintaining that the 'Sino-Soviet split', in keeping with his premise, was an artfully induced Western misperception. To laugh at this primitive, and in retrospect erroneous, assertion may be no less unwise *sub specie aeternitatis* than disqualifying Pythagoras as a mathematician for his belief in the transmigration of souls. Yet ever since then it became obligatory for even the most open-minded observers of totalitarian evolution to dissociate themselves publicly from Golitsyn, something I have been invited to do on several occasions. To be sure, any theory based on a claim to universality is difficult to accept rationally. But if political science is a science, it must allow room for Golitsyn's theory as a hypothesis and judge it solely on its effectiveness as a predictive tool, rather than some other, more emotive, merits or demerits.

The Oxford political scientist John Gray, adding in the obligatory disclaimer to a 1989 essay that he did not 'endorse Golitsyn's theories', was nonetheless fair-minded enough to include a long passage from Golitsyn's *New Lies for Old*.[4] Bearing in mind that the 'predictions for the next stage of Soviet development' were made by the author in 1983, it is worthwhile to read the passage in full and ponder the extent to which, in Gray's words, 'his expectations have been corroborated by events'. 'Political "liberalization" and "democratization"' in Moscow, wrote Golitsyn,

> would be spectacular and impressive. Formal pronouncements might

> be made about a reduction in the communist party's role; its monopoly would be apparently curtailed. An ostensible separation of powers between the legislative, the executive, and the judiciary might be introduced. The Supreme Soviet would be given greater apparent power and the president and deputies greater apparent independence. The posts of president of the Soviet Union and first secretary of the party might well be separated. The KGB would be "reformed". Dissidents at home would be amnestied; those in exile abroad would be allowed to return, and some would take up positions of leadership in government. Sakharov might be included in some capacity in the government or allowed to teach abroad. The creative arts and cultural and scientific organizations, such as the writers' unions and Academy of Sciences, would become apparently more independent, as would the trade unions. Political clubs would be opened to nonmembers of the communist party. Leading dissidents might form one or more alternative political parties. Censorship would be relaxed; controversial books, plays, films, and art would be published, performed, and exhibited. Many prominent Soviet performing artists now abroad would return to the Soviet Union and resume their professional careers. Constitutional amendments would be adopted to guarantee fulfillment of the provisions of the Helsinki agreements and a semblance of compliance would be maintained. There would be greater freedom for Soviet citizens to travel. Western and United Nations observers would be invited to the Soviet Union to witness the reforms in action....
>
> "Liberalization" in Eastern Europe would probably involve the return to power in Czechoslovakia of Dubcek and his associates. If it should be extended to East Germany, demolition of the Berlin Wall might even be contemplated.
>
> Western acceptance of the new "liberalization" as genuine would create favourable conditions for the fulfillment of communist strategy for the United States, Western Europe, and even, perhaps, Japan.

I do not want to belittle the predictive power of this hypothesis by noting that it originated already after Brezhnev's death. It is precisely because what is known in the West today as 'Gorbachev's perestroika' had been launched by his mentor Andropov during Brezhnev's last years that Golitsyn's analysis was borne out by events. Yet, inside Russia, roughly similar predictions had been made privately when I was a teenager, when Brezhnev's *ancien regime* was at its height and Andropov largely invisible.

My own criticism of Golitsyn's thinking, then, is not that it is outlandishly *outré* but that it is insufficiently analytical. Its weaknesses are those Golitsyn shares with Western Sovietologists, not those which have caused them to dismiss him. Thus, in the passage above, he mistakenly identifies a 'reduction in the communist party's role' with civic progress: its 'monopoly', he insists, would be curtailed only *apparently*, even as the global 'fulfillment of communist strategy' continued. Yet, as every Western Sovietologist can now prove, the role of the Communist Party in Russia, and even more plainly in Eastern Europe, has been *genuinely* curtailed. Does this mean, however, that the fulfilment of the totalitarian strategy continues no longer, or that the stretegy is any less global?

By placing Golitsyn in the first circle of Sovietology, a wise man's inferno by analogy with a fool's paradise, I pay tribute to both the courage of his convictions and his predictive successes as a political thinker. But so long as he shares conceptual weaknesses -- such as the misidentification of 'communist' ideology with totalitarianism's real methods and aims -- with Western 'anti-communists' like Professor Laqueur, he cannot be called a political scientist. As far as I know, the West has produced only one political scientist, George Orwell, in the seventy-three years of the totalitarian era.

The Anti-communist's Cobra

John Gray's essay mentioned above, 'Totalitarianism, Reform and Civil Society'[5], is one of the most impressive contributions to the Sovietological debate within this, its first circle: as Golitsyn will be remembered by future generations in one breath with the emigré Cassandras who preceded him, so it is easy to recognise in Gray a modern-day Eugene Lyons or Malcolm Muggeridge. Indeed, his essay is seminal in that its author focuses on the 'ominous parallels between the disinformation exercises of the NEP period' in the 1920s and the 'policies of *glasnost*' in the 1980s while exposing the cardinal weakness of Western Sovietological method with respect to 'the potential for strategic disinformation possessed and exercised by the Soviet regime'. As a result, he concludes, the Soviet regime 'can proceed with its program of modernizing its military forces while appearing to reduce its offensive capacity'.

Gray's intuition, fuelled by his scepticism with respect to the 'conventional methodology' of Soviet studies, is that developments like the 'dramatic collapse of the Communist monopoly on power' in Eastern Europe are 'tactical moves in a Soviet strategy of "reverse Finlandization"'. Yet this is a contradiction: surely if the 'collapse' was 'dramatic' because it was inadvertent, it could not have been a 'tactical move'. And why 'reverse' Finlandization? Here, it seems, Gray falls victim to the very methodology he decries, as he advances the notion that

> By comparison with the NEP period, the USSR now confronts far graver problems of ethnic conflict, nationalist and separatist tendencies, religious and fundamentalist movements, and environmental degradation.... Nor is it obvious or even plausible that infusions of Western credit can facilitate the resurrection of the USSR's senile industries.

The resolution of the apparent contradiction is thus suggested: though 'conceived as a ground deception', totalitarianism's 'extraordinarily risky' new initiatives will not reverse what Western Sovietology has characterized as an impending or occurring Soviet collapse. Hence the dramatic 'fall of communism' in Eastern Europe is a net gain for the West.

So ideology rears its head once more. Having braved the Sovietological consensus, Gray is nonetheless too fearful of fear to carry the argument through to its logical conclusion. The impending Soviet economic or general 'collapse' is, for him, a common ground of hope with the Sovietologists he derides. It is for this reason that he clings approvingly to the following quotation from James Sherr's *Soviet Power: The Continuing Challenge*:

> Whatever its ostensible purpose, the elimination of the market and the creation of a command economy has one clear consequence: the who, what, and how of economic relations is determined by planners, not by

> those who produce and consume. It is the structure of the system that demands this, not the unimaginativeness or selfishness of those involved. An enterprise director cannot do what he considers best for society since, without the market's signals, he cannot know what this is. He may know the difference between a tractor that works and one which does not, but he cannot know how many tractors are required, what sort of tractors to build, and where they are most needed.

'Best for society'? Like Gray, Sherr is too frightened by fear to postulate that the economic system of totalitarianism perfected by Stalin, 'state capitalism', has succeeded in segregating -- and flaunting -- *non-strategic* central planning with such sophistication that Western observers have never been able so much as to peek behind its picturesquely crumbling facade. Unfortunately for the West, in *strategic* areas this vaudeville of central planning where the totalitarian rulers determine what is 'best for society' down to the last bolt is a Sovietological myth.

One example will suffice. In 1939, when Stalin wanted to build a new fighter plane, he established *seventeen* design bureaux in competition with one another; each was fully capitalised to carry out research and each designer, staff member and file clerk was remunerated, even though it was known from the start that only one model would emerge from the competition, with sixteen others discarded; as a result, not one but three fighter planes (MiG-1, Yak-1 and Lag-1) came into being and laid the foundation of Soviet air power in a matter of months. The efficient economic system Stalin used is called an internal market.

Characteristically, it is tractors that come to Sherr's mind when he thinks of the glory of 'Western' economic competition and the splendour of 'Western' free enterprise. No doubt, Soviet tractors, in contrast to Soviet tanks, do not work. But as I write these lines I hear that it is Soviet MiGs that Switzerland has ordered, that Russia is years ahead of the West in military applications of space technology, that its production of weapons not in the West's arsenal, such as reload-refire ICBMs, has doubled within the last year, and that new submarines now added to its global fleet are the first to use titanium in their construction.

Reviewing Viktor Suvorov's latest book, a history of the Second World War entitled *Icebreaker*, for *The Times* I compared the author with Kant.[6] The revelatory quality of Suvorov's writing owes something to his past experiences as a tank commander, an officer in *spetsnaz* and a military intelligence operative. It owes more to the defector's intellect, trained, in particular, on the problem of allocation of strategic resources, including intellect, under totalitarianism. The emerging panorama of an hermetically closed, segregated strategic infrastructure demonstrates beyond doubt that Soviet 'state capitalism' relies on competition, not planning, to overtake the West with its 'private capitalism' whose incompatibility with strategic necessity was first outlined by Orwell in his essays. To dismiss Suvorov's prolegomena is, once again, to sink in the muddle of ideology: wicked 'communism' is the opposite of successful 'capitalism', 'capitalism' abhors 'planning' because anything but a free market means eventual 'economic collapse', therefore 'communism' must eventually 'collapse'. But not to dismiss them is, once again, to think the unthinkable: can it be that the 'command economy' visibly failing before Western eyes from the coal mines of Donets to the bakeries of Moscow is not, as it were, the real thing?

Thus the consensus prevails even against the bravest. Roger Scruton was among them when he wrote, on the op-ed page of *The Sunday Telegraph*[7], of 'arms control negotiations' past and present:

> When these began at Stalin's request, the Soviet Union was in a state of comparative military weakness. The Soviets had acquired atomic weapons; but they had no ability to strike at the United States, and would have been at the mercy of any Western Alliance that chose to dictate to them. After 40 years of arms control the situation is precisely the reverse. We now find ourselves at a disadvantage in almost every strategic field...

No better, or braver, summary of the West's diplomatic follies since Stalin's day than Scruton's words preceding my ellipsis is required. He continues, however, thus:

> ... and had it not been for the internal collapse of communism...

Mere inches away from the impossible! Indeed, to those observing these aerobatics it seems that Scruton has crashed on the common ground of hope, and only the distant roar of the engines keeps them from crying out in fear:

> ... which few foresaw, we should have lived henceforth in fear and trembling. Indeed, it is the military strength of the Soviet Union that causes us still to humour its leaders in the peculiar belief that this is the best way to encourage their reformist tendencies, and to bolster them against the 'hawks' that threaten at any moment to oust them from power.

No better, or braver, indictment of the West's political myopia since Andropov's day can be expected. But the pilot did touch the ground, for the 'internal collapse of communism' is at best an unproven assumption and at worst a damnable fiction.

The aces of intellectual pilotage likely to perform this trick are exceedingly few, as few perhaps as the fighter pilots who can manage the famous 'Pugachev's Cobra'. Like both Gray and Scruton, they are almost never Sovietologists by training. One exception is the veteran 'anti-communist' Brian Crozier, who recently replicated the feat in the scope of a letter to *The Times* as follows:

> Sir, You ask who, even two years ago, would have foreseen the demolition of the Berlin Wall ("Not without honour", leading article, October 16). The answer is Anatoly Golitsyn, in his book *New Lies for Old* (p. 340). Golitsyn defected in 1961, and his book was published in the UK in 1984, a year before Mikhail Gorbachev reached the top. As a former KGB deception specialist, Golitsyn also foresaw the return of Sakharov and Dubcek, the liberalisation in the Soviet Union and Eastern Europe. He didn't need a crystal ball to forecast the great deception exercise of the past few years.

Thus the brave scholar appeared to challenge the consensus view expressed by the *Times* leader writers as, 'for the first time since its inauguration in 1901, the Nobel committee awarded the peace prize to a communist head of state, Mikhail Gorbachev'. Yet Crozier's letter contained one other, last sentence:

> What he [Gorbachev] could not foresee was that the exercise would get out of control.
> Yours very truly, &c.[8]

And thus Crozier, determined to rebut the consensus, ended up doing nothing of the kind and, if anything, endorsed the leader writer's view that

> The weakness of the Soviet empire, the internal contradictions of communism, left him [Gorbachev] no choice but to permit Eastern Europe's liberation, to slow the nuclear arms race and mend fences with the West and, at home, to expand civil liberties and end the Communist Party's monopoly of power. Such cavilling is ungracious.... Who, six years ago, would have described as inevitable the Soviet withdrawal from Afghanistan...[9]

and so on.

Actually, *Pravda* described the Soviet withdrawal from Afghanistan as inevitable at the time of the invasion and on numerous occasions immediately thereafter (with the implied proviso that this would occur just as soon as its purpose was accomplished, which is precisely what happened). Nor did the leader writer's dimly second-hand supposition that, along with Andropov, Brezhnev was Gorbachev's 'patron' inspire confidence: at the risk of trivialising the matter, this is like saying that Margaret Thatcher owed her decade in power to the patronage of Ted Heath. But such cavilling is even more ungracious, I suppose. My point here is, once again, that so long as both the consensus-monger and his critic are 'anti-communists', the factual floundering of one and the scholarly expertise of the other are not, fundamentally, at odds. Both are blinkered by ideology and unable to see beyond the great wonder of the age, that the baddest communist on earth turned out to be an anti-communist: not as good as either of them, of course, but give him a Nobel Peace Prize, or at least some credit. 'Would Yuri Andropov have presided over such changes?' asked the consensus-monger of *The Times* with rhetorical abandon. Now, there's a communist baddie for you! At the very least the critic must logically concede that yes, Andropov was a communist baddie.

While it is quite clear to me that had Yuri Andropov lived for a decade longer Soviet policy changes would have been identical to those the West has now witnessed and, if anything, even more spectacular, conjectural assertions of this kind obviously cannot be proven. What can be proven, however, is that Andropov was the greatest 'anti-communist' since Stalin, who was the greatest 'anti-communist' of them all if only by virtue of his clear understanding of ideology's function in a brave new world that awards its criminals no prizes unless whole nations are their victims.

More Dissidents

My ongoing review of Western Sovietological opinion has shown that no segment of the Right-to-Left 'political spectrum' has a monopoly on insight or delusion; moreover, today it is the long-established 'anti-communist' Right that is rather less likely to rise above the deceptions of Soviet ideological change[10]. Like dissidents in Russia, those who dare to challenge the consensus come from all walks of life; they may have the will, but lack the analytical skill to break out of ideology's confines existing within a culture which totalitarianism, from the very start, has been shrewd enough to have in common with its once and future inmates. These Western 'dissidents', then, populate what I have called the first circle of Sovietology's intellectual inferno. More names must now be named.

The anonymous *Times* editorialist of 1990, in applauding the Nobel committee's sycophancy, represented the consensus. His anonymous predecessor of exactly three years earlier, booing the same committee's award of the prize to President Arias of Costa Rica in tribute to 'his work for peace in Central America', opposed it. Since the appearance of a leader in a major national newspaper is one yardstick by which the amplitude of the consensus may be measured, the reader will note how much that dimension has shrunk in only three years:

> The award is another example of the way in which signatories of peace treaties are widely regarded as automatically contributing to peace.... By these standards, Molotov and Ribbentrop would have qualified for the award had their handiwork not been followed by war so quickly. The Churchill of the 1930s, who believed that peace could be secured only by Britain and France rearming, would not have qualified. In fact, after the war which his treaty helped unleash, Molotov was indeed recommended for a Nobel. So, at various stages in their careers, were Mussolini and Stalin.[11]

My surmise concerning the identity of the authors of the two leading articles is perhaps irrelevant, despite my abiding desire to name names for posterity's sake. What is relevant is that, by today's standard, yesterday's leader is not mere ungracious cavilling but what is known in official Soviet language as an ugly provocation.

The Times, in 1987, was by no means 'the most conservative newspaper in Britain'. A Mori poll in that year showed 59% of its readership voting Tory and 28% for the Alliance, as compared with 78% and 8% for the *Financial Times*, 69% and 21% for the *Daily Telegraph* (31% and 35% for the *Independent*, 22% and 37% for the *Guardian*, to spread these figures into a 'political spectrum' of non-Left opinion).[12] That no such 'provocations' came from elsewhere does indeed suggest that it is individual thinkers and not representatives of political or quasipolitical groupings who may be looked to for signs of meaningful dissent against the hegemony of consensus.

'Provocation' stirred again at *The Times* in the form of David Hart. Admittedly, Hart is a Tory, yet one who is widely perceived within his own party as a 'maverick' without a political future. On at least three op-ed occasions Hart was able publicly to pierce the consensus. In 1987, in 'Radical is as radical does':

> The proposed INF missiles treaty will increase European exposure to the massive Soviet conventional, chemical and biological superiority.

> President Reagan seems intent on trying to rush into other even more significant nuclear weapons agreements, principally for domestic political reasons. At present, the government is cutting defence spending by 5 percent in real terms. In the atmosphere of new detente that is breaking out it will find it hard to explain to the electorate that it needs to increase defence spending again. Yet it will have to, if it is not to expose Europe and this country to the risk of Soviet blackmail.[13]

In 1988, in 'Selling out Afghanistan':

> Despite its superficial attractions, a Soviet troop withdrawal is not at all in the interest of the West unless it is unconditional or accompanied by a settlement that offers a realistic hope that the Afghans will be able to settle their own affairs.... Nor is a defective settlement in the interest of Western political leaders. If such a settlement leads to a permanent communist government in Kabul, Western public opinion might well wonder why their leaders have sold out the very people they have been supporting so loudly for the past nine years.[14]

In 1989, in 'Moscow's Trojan horse':

> Western political leaders should spend less time wondering what kind of compromise can be achieved with Chancellor Kohl on short-range nuclear missiles and more time asking themselves why West Germany has arrived at its present political condition and what steps they can take to stop it acting as a conduit for mounting and skillfully applied Soviet pressure on Nato....
>
> Many observers have been puzzled by Gorbachev's much-vaunted "new thinking" in foreign policy and are wondering what it portends. His determination to use old principles for influencing Western Europe is entirely consistent with traditional Soviet practice. His methods are, however, much more sophisticated.
>
> Perhaps that is what "new thinking" amounts to.[15]

Hart's brilliantly predictive pieces of analysis were amplified on the same page by another dissident who deserves to be mentioned in this connection, Gerald Frost. In August 1987 Frost wrote in *The Times* that

> During the period in which the West has sought to control nuclear weapons through bilateral agreement the balance of forces has steadily improved in the Soviets' favour, however measured, forcing the US to make dramatic changes to its strategy and the kind of weapons it deploys. Under the influence of the peace movement and of political leaders who wished to give arms agreements a more simple and persuasive rationale, the public has come to expect the talks to achieve cuts in nuclear force levels and an improvement in East-West relations. Both expectations have been thwarted. A returning realization that the Soviet Union presents the same threat to the West as it did before means that improvements in the international climate have been short-lived.
>
> Apart from these wider concerns, the "zero-zero" option will expose Europe to the considerable intimidatory power of the Soviet Union's conventional and chemical weapons, to nuclear systems outside the scope of the talks and to new systems which the Soviets may be now deploying.[16]

In the end the reader may reflect that Frost's early view cannot claim to be more than a word of caution, substantively not unlike the *Independent*'s vague advice, proffered at the time, 'to remain somewhat sceptical about *glasnost* and *perestroika*'.[17] It was, however, expanded by its author a year later, in the first essay on record to discuss in detail, albeit cautiously, the turning of Margaret Thatcher. Entitled 'Margaret and Mikhail: The Odyssey of an Odd Couple', it addressed the question of how Britain was distracted from the 'task of seeking to create a credible structure of European defence', concluding:

> To be sure, that is not as exciting a task as assisting an heroic Soviet leader to reverse the Bolshevik Revolution, but it happens to be one which needs to be done.[18]

In the wise, even if somewhat ambiguously deployed, irony of that observation one detects the rumbling of an analytical thought qualitatively different from the *Independent*'s well-meaning platitude.

Another dissident would soon echo these voices in the op-ed pages of *The Times*. In contrast to Hart, this 'maverick' did not belong to the Conservative Party and subsequently proved that he could not belong to his own party either. 'It is difficult to resist the thought', Peter Stothard wrote in *The Times* of the SDP conference in Torquay in September 1988, 'that, deep in his heart, David Owen is not naturally a man of any party'. Perhaps for that reason, Stothard implied in his profile[19], what the Torquay audience heard

> was a fine political speech. It would be good, for example, to hear Sir Geoffrey Howe point out so forthrightly Mr Gorbachev's admiration for Lenin, the KGB's for *perestroika*, and the risks for isolationism in the US.

At the time, my own efforts to publish an article entitled 'Doing business with the wrong men', an outline of the history of the coup by the secret-police apparatus which brought Andropov and his successor to power, came to nought at *The Times*. A mere year of hardening consensus later, a renewed attempt to have the article published in the 'more conservative' *Sunday Telegraph* by drawing the editors' attention to Dr Owen's intuitions elicited epithets like 'barmy': how else to describe a man who puts his own perception of historical truth before the earthly reward of political power?

Let the reader turn a blind eye to the word 'Communism' in the passage below -- an analytical weakness which Dr Owen shares with his fellow inmates of the first circle -- and judge whether or not his insights can be dismissed by anyone with a taste for historical truth:

> In the late 1970s it became clear to us in the West that a radical group was emerging from within the KGB which was arguing to change the arthritic, centralized and bureaucratic methods of conducting Soviet economic and foreign policy. They were not liberals, but hard-headed realists....
>
> As yet, there has been no sign that the KGB as a whole is disillusioned with the Gorbachev package. In a sense, why should they be? Reconstruction, with its emphasis on decentralization and greater accountability, is aimed at increasing Soviet wealth, without which the worldwide projection of Soviet Communism will forever be stunted. More public discussion of ideas and information is a small price to pay

> in a closed society if it generates economic growth. Democratization, provided it is strictly limited, as it is, to increasing the citizen's interest and involvement in the political process, need not challenge the power structures of Soviet society.
>
> Of course, the KGB is watching the whole exercise like a hawk, only too well aware that it could feed fissiparous tendencies, and start to challenge the basis of its power. But provided the process is carefully controlled the KGB believes that the new style is beneficial in pursuing its major foreign policy objectives: namely the denuclearization of Europe on Soviet terms, and the extension of Soviet influence in Third World countries....
>
> At any moment, we can expect a Soviet initiative proposing extensive reductions in conventional weaponry. Bulldozers in the full gaze of the world's television cameras may soon be let loose on the Berlin Wall. Eduard Shevarnadze has already felt able, in Bonn of all places, to tell us that Moscow would never permit Nato to fulfill its intention, announced well in advance of the INF agreement, to modernize some of its existing nuclear arsenals.[20]

Thus, *inter alia*, in spite of the *Times* editorialist's later admonition against 'ungracious cavilling', it is quite clear that somebody had predicted the future of the Berlin Wall on the very same page of the very same newspaper. But after almost three years of increasingly restrictive consensus, obviously no newspaper editor could be expected to show his own ungraciously cavillous side by pointing this out to the leader writer. As for the KGB's enthusiasm for *perestroika*, especially in Eastern Europe, Dr Owen's fears were confirmed in February 1989 by a programme made for Scottish Television by Jimmy Reid, leader of the 1971 Clyde shipyard occupation, under the title 'Reid About Poland'.[21] Analyzing, in classic labour-management terms, the appropriation of the 'Solidarity' movement and the subsequent accommodation of Moscow by Lech Walesa, Reid timed his diagnosis of the great betrayal to Margaret Thatcher's visit to Poland.

Since the spring of 1988, when Reid's revelations were aired, the Western consensus of Sovietological opinion has become an automaton intolerant of dissent, even as public debate on the subject has narrowed. The pronouncements of veteran 'anti-communists', once again disoriented by the ideological change in Moscow, are a tangle of self-contradiction and self-deception. Consider this eminently reasonable forecast:

> In the worst case, we might be on the verge of the virtual disintegration of Nato, with West Germany seeking some accommodation with the Soviet Union and the rest of Western Europe effectively "Finlandized".

Yet this observation, within the scope of a single op-ed article by 'a vice president of the European Atlantic Group and the author of *Defence of the Realm*', is followed by another:

> If Reagan's legacy is to be, as now seems likely, the emergence of a strong, secure and confident Soviet Union, Mrs Thatcher's might well be the emergence of a strong, secure and confident Europe.[22]

It remains unclear whether Alun Chalfont realises that the 'strong, secure' totalitarianism will favour a 'strong, secure' Europe only if Europe continues to disarm, and that this is precisely what his 'worst case' scenario is all about.

It may be suggested that the notional 'circle' of opposition to the ruling consensus which I have thought necessary to identify in these pages is arbitrary, artificial and ultimately unreal. Not so. Today, as forty or seventy years ago, there exists physically and functions intellectually in the West an entity called the Russian emigration, with its own Sovietologists, its own periodical press and its own culture. It may be added that were it not for the presence of this entity, the West would not know a hundredth of what it has learned since 1917 about Soviet totalitarianism. Today, as forty or seventy years ago, the Sovietological debate in the pages of *La Pensée Russe* (Paris), *Kontinent* (Munich) or *Time and We* (New York) is conducted on a plane of fact and logic wholly absent from its Western media counterpart. Thus Anatoly Golitsyn is not a prophet who happened to be Russian, but an average participant in the emigreé debate who happened to be a high-ranking KGB defector and was able to become at least audible in the West. The circle of nay-sayers

I have portrayed here is merely a part of that submerged iceberg of non-consensus Sovietological opinion visible to the British media, visible because its members are English speakers and writers. To observe the whole submerged structure of what amounts to a school of Sovietological literacy, and to understand its relationship with Western 'dissidence', all one need do is learn Russian.[23]

Before taking leave of the first circle to glimpse the inferno's inner recesses, I should note that, not being a political party, the dissidents who comprise it can neither win nor lose. As individuals, they seek after political truth as men once strove for personal salvation. Thus, in December 1987, two American women, school teachers in Fountain Hill, Arkansas, refused to require their pupils to invite Mikhail Gorbachev to see their town on his visit to the United States, a courtesy made politically expedient by the national consensus of editorial opinion and ruled mandatory by the local superintendent of schools. How, in the end, could Mrs Jane Graves and Mrs Kay Hammil have hoped to profit by their defiance? 'If the students had been given a choice, it would have been different', said one. The other did not believe that she should 'encourage my children to make a hero of a man who is out to dominate the world'.[24] Both were promptly sacked, and I record their names here to illustrate that at any social level striving after political truth is a necessary but not sufficient condition for overturning the consensus.

By and large, the effectiveness of the first circle's impact on the West's strategy or foreign policy has been similar to that made by the brave Arkansas teachers: unwilling to deceive themselves and others into the triumphalism of their 'anti-communist' peers ('*The Soviets blinked*', Ronald Reagan reportedly wrote in his diary on 27 October 1987, generously peppering his later memoirs with the phrase[25]), they were outmanoeuvred by events and lost much of their local influence. What they lacked was a comprehensive, coherent programme of historical analysis, without which their nay-saying sounded like the warmed-over cold-war hysteria which their opponents always said it was.

And when the dust of debate had settled, it transpired that Lord

Chalfont, a peer of the realm writing under the lion and unicorn of *The Times*, did not do more than two obscure school teachers a few hours' drive from Little Rock, Arkansas: he defended freedom of choice, proposed a worst-case scenario and put his fate in God's hands.

What Really Happened

On 2 November 1988, when I sent off my jarring analysis of recent events to the first of several newspapers, Soviet totalitarianism was preparing to celebrate yet another anniversary of its victory over democracy in Russia. Western electorates knew less than ever about the identity of Soviet rulers and the nature of their rule. The course of thought and action which the leaders of political parties in the West had been empowered to pursue with respect to the Kremlin was based, more than ever before, on blind assumptions.

Since 12 March 1985, when Mikhail Gorbachev became General Secretary, every interpretative model used by Western analysts to assess subsequent events had been based on one such assumption: whoever bears the title of General Secretary may be presumed to have triumphed over his competitors in the power struggle and established himself as the ruler of the Soviet state. The assumption was born of misguided hindsight and handed down through the decades. What it discounts is the truth that Stalin had seized on the title precisely because it was inconspicuous, even demeaning; held real, later total, power for some fifteen years before deigning to accept a grander title; and accepted one on the eve of the war only after the linchpin of his global strategy, the Nazi-Soviet Pact negotiated by a figurehead 'head of state', was safely in place. Just as Orwell believed that a democracy's military establishment always prepares for the last war, I believe that its Sovietologists expect the new Stalin to smoke a pipe and sport a moustache.

Since the policies which the new General Secretary came to advocate, both domestically and internationally, appeared radical to many, the assumption seemed irresistibly plausible. What made it so popular, however, was the perceived overall direction of these policies, eagerly regarded in the West as a promise of 'fundamental change', coupled with specific diplomatic initiatives, generously interpreted as a partial fulfilment of that promise. I shall address the motive behind these Western misperceptions later. For now, one need only recall that here the parallel with Stalin is obvious: even in Russia, Stalin's launch of what he called *perestroika* in 1932 earned him the reputation (among Russian writers and artists, for instance) of a liberator (from, for instance, Russophobic 'communist' activists in charge of culture, forcibly promulgating literary experiment and abstract art), indeed a 'saviour' ('Socialist Realism', unveiled along with other cultural reforms in Eastertide, was viewed as a return to the freedom of conventional self-expression unfettered by modernist mandate). In the West, such enthusiasms were common well into the late 1930s, as these were further fuelled by 'Stalin's Constitution', with its guaranteed delivery of ballot-boxes to the bedside of the infirm and related paraphernalia of political reform (which by then had an equally enthusiastic reception inside Russia only because already accompanied by mass terror).

Meanwhile, the new General Secretary's presumed opponents within the Soviet oligarchy seemed to encroach on his power publicly only to be beaten back, just as publicly, to the satisfaction of Western observers now increasingly committed to their key assumptions: that (1) Gorbachev was well on his way to having absolute power, like Stalin, and that (2) absolute power would not corrupt him absolutely, because (3) unlike Stalin he was not a 'communist' dictator. As we shall see, all three of these assumptions were flawed, but by the time Ronald Reagan visited Moscow to sign the INF treaty endorsed by a majority of U.S. Senators before they had read it[26], *glasnost, perestroika* and *demokratizatsiya* on everyone's lips were widely perceived as sufficient evidence of both Gorbachev's power and his intent to use it for the good of mankind.

The words in question, however, had been first used publicly to denote policy initiatives subsequently associated with Gorbachev exactly three years before I sent off my article: in November 1985, in a Kremlin speech on the anniversary of its 'Great October Socialist Revolution' dominating the next day's edition of *Pravda*. Mikhail Gorbachev, General Secretary since March, sat in the audience, applauding dutifully in all the right places. The speaker was Viktor Chebrikov, head of the KGB.

Chebrikov's speech passed unnoticed in the Western press because few outside the very centre of power in the Soviet oligarchy could have known that November how great a role the concepts Chebrikov was introducing would play in years to come. Gorbachev, for one, did not know it or knew it only in the vaguest possible sense: neither *glasnost* nor any other buzzword of today is to be found in the index to the 1986 edition of his collected articles and speeches, approved for publication in December 1985. In fact, as even Western observers now reluctantly acknowledge, many of his pronouncements during his first year 'in power' as General Secretary would have qualified him a year later as a die-hard 'Kremlin conservative'.

It was not until 1986 that Gorbachev became, in the eyes of a hopeful West, the dominant 'liberal' of his 'administration', perpetually fighting a 'conservative opposition in the Kremlin', an opposition always losing yet never fully defeated. In retrospect, the verisimilitude of that public performance may be said to have owed something to the underlying reality of power play. At the time, however, the only relevant reality -- and the only one ignored by Western observers as their 'Kremlinological' theories grew more convoluted -- was that while the Mutt-and-Jeff routine did indeed star Gorbaligachev, this two-headed figurehead was in the employ of a higher authority, which had devised and subsequently sponsored the performance.

Why this is so must be self-evident *a priori*. Every trial lawyer knows better than to ask a witness in court a question the answer to which he has never heard. Every totalitarian oligarch knows better than to engage in public debate without the tacit consent of whoever is actually in power. Thus as Stalin-Zinoviev-Bukharin rallied against Trotsky, Stalin-Bukharin rallied against Zinoviev, and Stalin rallied against Bukharin accused of supporting Trotsky-Zinoviev, to the outsider it might have seemed that the struggle evolved spontaneously; yet Stalin remained a constant of power throughout and is understood to have devised and subsequently sponsored the entire performance as only real power can. Despite this, in the mid-1930s as in the mid-1980s, the West found itself dependent, intellectually and politically, on the course of a public performance whose outcome had in reality been predetermined a decade earlier.

By 1985 the authority at the epicentre of power in the Soviet oligarchy for the first time in history was the KGB. Available evidence suggests that the secret-police apparatus seized power, as Khrushchev expected it would on Stalin's death, under the ailing Brezhnev, when Yuri Andropov was at its head. Western intelligence analysts, not to mention the press, may perhaps be forgiven for knowing nothing of the coup until late 1980, long after the new regime had invisibly concentrated its power in the Politburo in Andropov's hands. In the autumn of 1980, however, when time came for that power to be felt, the newcomers began a campaign of intimidation against the old regime which, like all intimidation, had to be visible if it was to be effective. 4 October 1980 is the date on which the ignorance of Western intelligence analysts, Sovietologists and even Moscow correspondents became inexcusable. Yet it was to continue for a full decade.

On 21 October, 1980, Petr Masherov, First Secretary of Byelorussia, candidate member of the Politburo since 1966 and bearer of seven Orders of Lenin, was to become a full member of the Politburo. On 4 October, Masherov 'tragically perished', according to *Pravda*, 'in a car accident'. A totally unknown provincial named Gorbachev became a full member in Masherov's stead by virtue of being a personal protegé of Andropov. This was the first lethal car accident in Soviet history involving a personage of that rank: elaborate precautions of a kind only a totalitarian state can implement are standard procedure, guaranteeing total safety. An 'epidemic' of car accidents followed, however, involving other Brezhnev favourites in high places including Nikolai Suslov, Central Committee member and Second Secretary in Leningrad, slated to replace Grigory

Romanov, an 'Andropov man', in Leningrad and later in the Politburo. By 1982, the rash of premature deaths -- another candidate Politburo member from Byelorussia, a chairman of Georgia's Council of Ministers, a First Secretary of Tajikistan, a Party secretary in the Tatar region, another in the Yakut region -- amounted to a show of the newcomers' muscle.

To the same end, it was first rumoured and then announced publicly in early 1982 that 'stolen diamonds' had been found in the flat of Brezhnev's daughter, while her husband Yuri Churbanov, Deputy Minister of the Interior, was arrested and charged with 'corruption' in a legal farce of an investigation straight from the 1930s known as the 'trial of an era' which continued until 1988. Needless to say, 'contrary to a previous announcement', as *The Times* reported, 'only the beginning and end of the trial' were 'open to the public' or, as *The New York Times* put it even more innocently, 'Soviet reporters and selected members of the public' were 'permitted to attend the remaining sessions'[27].

Galina Brezhnev's lover, Boris Buryatse, died in prison on the night of his arrest, as did two of Churbanov's 'accomplices'. General Semyon Tsvigun, Deputy Chairman of the KGB and Brezhnev's brother-in-law, committed suicide or was suicided, whereupon on 21 January 1981 Andropov and Gorbachev signed the newspaper obituaries alongside senior members of the KGB leadership (an unprecedented display of concern in that it publicly revealed their identities). Interior Minister Nikolai Shchelokov was charged with corruption as well: his wife threw herself or was thrown to her death from a window, and shortly thereafter he shot himself or was shot with a hunting gun while wearing full military regalia. Arrests, prosecutions and convictions dragged on until 1988, when the 'trial of an era' finally opened and the city of Brezhnevsk changed its name. Brezhnev's private secretary, Gennady Brovin, was among the last to be convicted and imprisoned.

If these acts of terror seem random, this is because the campaign of intimidation against the old regime was just that, and not part of a scheme to win power. Power had changed hands at the top long before the campaign began, and now all that remained was for the sprawling executive organism to feel its sting and fall in with the new master's line. The above facts are only a few necessarily random pieces of a huge subterraneous mosaic. Its complete outline may never emerge.

What put total power in Andropov's hands even before Brezhnev died in November 1982 was his own fifteen years of total power over the secret-police apparatus. It will be recalled that Stalin changed his police chiefs with almost hygienic detachment. By contrast, Brezhnev's precautions proved inadequate. When Chebrikov, Andropov's 'special assistant' from 1969 to 1981, became KGB chief on Brezhnev's death, it became clear that the post of 'special assistant' had been invented by Andropov in order to circumvent his second in command, installed by Brezhnev as one of such precautions. Vladimir Kryuchkov, who later replaced Chebrikov at the KGB's helm, was among the loyal deputies Chebrikov had inherited from Andropov. Shortly after his elevation in 1988, *U.S. News & World Report* identified Kryuchkov, KGB station chief in New York until 1978, as 'the source of mysterious rumors circulated in the Soviet Union in the late 1970s that implicated the family of then party boss Leonid Brezhnev in shady financial deals'.[28]

Andropov's enthronement in the Politburo and the KGB pogrom of the Brezhnevite leadership raised no eyebrows in the West. When, during the November festivities in 1982, that morning's customary Politburo gallery of portraits excluded the Brezhnevite Kirilenko, for instance, no Western observer saw fit to reflect that the decision to dump a Politburo member like so much rubbish could only have been taken by someone with absolute control at the top. Instead, Western media greeted Andropov's enthronement with news of his taste for Scotch whisky, American jazz and Western democracy generally. As we shall see, this was based not entirely on deliberate KGB disinformation. Yet at the time, as we have already seen, the big story was clearly elsewhere.

After the death of his mentor Andropov in 1984, Chebrikov did not rush to have himself elected General Secretary *or even a member of the Politburo.* I have no doubt that he had ample opportunity to do so, since the secret-police apparatus which had won the whole power war for Andropov did not need to win so much as a battle of succession for his heir. The West's attention was diverted by the 'succession problem' under Chernenko. Meanwhile, Chebrikov's apparatus forged a winning strategy behind the scenes by grooming Gorbachev (and Ligachev, for that matter) for 'leadership'. In one of the rare slip-ups of Kremlin information control in 1988, *Pravda* printed Ligachev's party conference speech (attacking Boris Yeltsin, a PR man who had come to believe his own press releases and got carried away), without deleting Ligachev's admission that Gorbachev became General Secretary 'owing' first and foremost to Chebrikov. Yet when Gorbachev became General Secretary, it will be recalled, Chebrikov *was not even a member of the Politburo.*

In Western terms this is roughly equivalent to George Bush admitting in his inaugural address, a traditional showcase of democratic pieties, that he became president owing first and foremost to Brown Brothers Harriman, his family bankers. Yet no Western 'newspaper of record' grasped the enormity of Ligachev's admission. Significantly, when Chebrikov made himself a Politburo member and promoted Ligachev to the rank of Gorbachev's foil, at the April 1985 Plenum, among the subjects stressed by the new General Secretary was the need for control of the Soviet -- and therefore, of course, Western -- press, whose 'effectiveness increases considerably when [relevant] authorities render it [timely] help and support'.

General Chebrikov continued to remain behind the scenes, and the Soviet -- and therefore Western -- press did not violate his privacy even when, in an unprecedented development reminiscent of Stalin's innovative redefinition of his 'secretarial' role, in October 1988 he became head of the Politburo's new 'commission' on police and legality, effectively absorbing the Interior Ministry, along with its troops and the entire machinery of Soviet 'law', into the KGB force (whose own purely *military* capabilities, incidentally, had already been a match for any country with the possible exception of the

United States, France and Britain). On the face of it, the 'commission' belonged to the Politburo, yet soon after the last of the incredulous editors rejected my article in early 1989 it began to seem that it was the Politburo which belonged to the KGB's 'commission'. This, of course, would have made any editor incredulous: to doubt the significance of 'General Secretary' is unorthodox, to claim that the KGB is the state is 'barmy', but to suggest that the Politburo itself, Soviet Russia's mother and apple pie, could be a mere ornament, is as preposterous as suggesting that Stalin wanted to eradicate 'communism' long before Walter Laqueur came to loathe it. The Politburo's influence, to be sure, was then just beginning to wane, and what I predicted in early 1989 did not begin to take place until a year later, or 22 January 1990 to be precise.

In the interim, in a September 1989 'reshuffle', none other than Chebrikov's loyal deputy Kryuchkov, bypassing candidate-member status, took hold of his erstwhile superior's Politburo seat. Whether he had overthrown his boss or accommodated him is not immediately obvious, yet perhaps less important than what is: KGB's power over the Politburo only increased in that interim. Significantly, while Chebrikov, safely aboard the Politburo, allowed someone else to fill his KGB post, Kryuchkov made no such error and wisely hung on to the levers of power. Chebrikov receded into the background, while Gorbachev, in his fifth year as General Secretary, continued to trounce 'conservative' rivals in the open. The influence exercised by the KGB upon Gorbachev and in his behalf remained the chief guarantee of his political survival, and by 22 January 1990, certainly with Kryuchkov's help and possibly with Chebrikov's acquiescence, Gorbachev had indeed become a new Stalin.

Or more than a Stalin, for on that day Gorbachev made clear to the Politburo what even Stalin never made explicit: that it was ornamental, and that the General Secretary could proclaim himself Party Chairman. The breathtaking audacity of this, to Western eyes bureaucratically subtle, distinction was entirely lost on the West. Western media, following Western intelligence analysts, habitually refer to the 'General Secretary of the Communist Party', a title that has never existed. The General Secretary is a secretary of the Party's Central Committee, whose authority had long ago been supplanted by the Politburo's. The 'political party' which began its days as a minor political party, RSDRP/b/ (Russian Social-Democratic Workers' Party /bolsheviks/), could obviously never have had a Party Chairman because it would have been clear that he was the dictator, and an oligarch who eyed such a post in, say, 1922 would have had his eyes put out by his fellow oligarchs. The General Secretary, on the other hand, was accountable to the Central Committee, and when that grew too numerous, to the Politburo. Like the oligarch Lenin, or Stalin while he was still an oligarch, from 1922 to 1926, from 1985 to 1990 Gorbachev had been accountable -- at least nominally, since real power already lay elsewhere -- to the Politburo, and even, by tradition admittedly emptied of meaning, to the Central Committee and the Party as a whole. Long after Stalin became a dictator, he continued to wear oligarchic garb and maintain oligarchic courtesies. By contrast, Gorbachev threatened to proclaim himself Party Chairman, which meant that even in theory he would no longer be accountable to the Politburo (if it so much as survived), not to mention the Central Committee (a Politburo rubber-stamp since long ago) of the Communist Party (which could now, for all it mattered, be renamed 'National Party', as Stalin hoped it would be one day).

Quite openly, Gorbachev became a dictator.[29] On 13 February 1990, *Pravda* carried the final version of the 'Platform of the Central Committee of the CPSU for the 28th Congress of the Party'. This document trumpeted, for all who had ears to hear, that 'It is proposed to elect at the Congress a Chairman of the CPSU and his assistants'. The 'proposal', which could only have emerged from the meeting of 22 January, seemed to have been initialled by the Politburo's members in the same trembling hand with which Stalin's Bolshevik victims initialled their confessions.

The Congress in question was still months away when Gorbachev's option -- to do away with the Politburo openly -- became official. By mid-July, when the Congress convened, it transpired that Gorbachev would not pursue the option which had been openly his for six months, since mid-February, and would rather continue being 'elected' the 'President' he had been 'appointed'.[30] Perhaps he had learned from his old patron Chebrikov's example, or had been advised by his new patron Kryuchkov to learn, that the taking of titles, posts and positions of power does not keep one in power as effectively as the option of taking them at one's will.

The irony attendant on the events was that the absurd, indeed inconceivable, Western misnomer made it seem logical that a 'party secretary' (by analogy, perhaps, with a corporate secretary) should rise to become 'party chairman' (by analogy with a corporate chairman). Cheering Gorbachev on in his struggle with the 'conservative' opposition to become a kind of 'liberal' Stalin, the Western press hardly noticed the proposed 'promotion' or saw it as an incremental career advance. It was, in fact, as qualitative a leap from oligarchy to dictatorship as that made by Stalin, with the difference that in Gorbachev's case, thanks to the KGB's backing, it was made overtly and in a matter of months rather than years. The KGB takeover under Brezhnev was a coup, yet it was still an inter-oligarchic coup. On 22 January 1990 the new oligarchy openly solidified into dictatorship.

As my last 'Kremlinological' (rather an obsolete term, incidentally, as the levers of power are now elsewhere and 'Lubyankological' is at least equally meaningful) reconstruction demonstrates, Soviet political realities have tracked Western perceptions of those realities without, nevertheless, becoming any more benign in the process. Ruling political parties and governments in Western democracies — communicating with policy analysts in Moscow through the Western media, whose reports, refracting Soviet media reports, are Moscow's chief gauge of Western public opinion -- have indeed helped Gorbachev to become a dictator. We may therefore turn to Russia's newfound freedom of expression, in the light of Gorbachev's early interest in giving the Soviet media timely help and support.

In the words of Sergei Grigoryants, dissident editor of the magazine *Glasnost*, already by July 1987 Andropov's initiative now associated with Gorbachev had taken shape as 'KGB-sown democracy and *glasnost*'. This view is echoed by another Moscow dissident, Valery Senderov, describing in the emigre magazine *Kontinent* the methodology of 'choking' genuine opposition with 'weeds', spontaneous provocations harmless for the regime yet useful for identifying such opposition. The overall effect is a polyphony of harmless oppositionism, an illusion of diversity that can easily mean all things to all people inside and outside Russia.

Who was right, *Glasnost*-readers in Moscow or *glasnost*-enthusiasts in the West? Corroboration of Senderov's view, in particular, comes from evidence that even before Andropov's coup under Brezhnev succeeded, the KGB had gone to great lengths to court the social science community within the Soviet Academy of Sciences and in the end secured their cooperation in a kind of 'closed' research institute, or private think-tank, of the KGB leadership. Admittedly, the KGB's early interest in clinical psychology got rather a bad name in the West as the result of its innovative use of madhouses, but such were Brezhnev's clumsy ways and few in the West connected Andropov with that protracted experiment. A similarly keen interest in applied sociology, on the other hand, could only have brought him accolades. That interest first became known in the West as long ago as 1977, when *The Washington Post* published an article by Boris Rabbot, a Soviet emigré who had personally advised Andropov, whom he described as 'the Politburo's most intelligent member', while working on secret sociological studies of the population.

Rabbot's account betrayed the initial, domestic rationale for what would later become known as '*glasnost*': sociologists and psychologists advising the KGB had explained that they could not 'study' or manipulate a frightened and defensive 'electorate' or populace. Andropov must have known equally well that until the KGB had total power no experiment on such a scale could be permissible or safe. But when at last he came to power, blueprints of domestic *glasnost* were already on the drawing board.

'Look at the major Western media with their freedom of the press and expression', Andropov's intermediaries with the Academy of Sciences might have advised him. 'What have they uncovered since

1917, at any rate quickly enough to make a difference, that was actually harmful to our empire?' 'Nothing', Andropov might have agreed. 'Given timely help and support from us, our major media can be just as open. The more open they are, the more their Western counterpart will take them at face value. And if there are minor, dissident media voices in the West, who listens to them? Nobody. We too can allow minor, dissident media voices. Of course, if one of these should become troublesome we will deal with it administratively: paper shortage, tax evasion, accidental death. But if one of them should reveal a state secret, there are plenty of articles in our criminal code to show him where the crab winters.'

'I take your point', Andropov might have mused. 'And my own experience as overseer of the Hungarian "thaw", when I was Soviet Ambassador to Hungary, allows me to put your advice in a larger strategic context. I came to Budapest in 1953. For three years we instigated liberalization, which was reversed in a matter of days in 1956, whereupon I was promoted to supervise new "thaws" as Chief of Liaison with Socialist Countries, I think we called it. Well, by the time I became head of the KGB in 1967 -- it was just about then that we dropped the "K" for "Committee" on our shoulder-straps, as one day we will surely drop the "B" for "Security" so that only the "G" for "State" will remain — liberalization was again in full bloom all over the place. And again we reversed it, in a matter of days and with minimal casualties, in 1968. Yet the West's optimism kept up with their reluctance to pay taxes, or spend on defence, and for a decade every American president hugged that oaf Brezhnev in the hope of seeing more liberalization. Why not give them something even better, something permanent or permanently moving toward permanence, something their anti-communist businessmen, politicians and journalists can witness as a fundamental break with communism?

'My premise is simple. Periods of liberalization -- during which arms-control deals keep their military potential from developing and technology transfer allows our strategic infrastructure to grow -- are long. On the other hand, our strikes to restore order, at targets easily monitored by us because liberalization flushes out the malcontents and brings dissent into the open, are quick and quickly forgotten. And the more powerful our strategic infrastructure, the more quickly will these mishaps be forgotten. Because the West is its public opinion, made up of individual human beliefs, and it is only human to forgive the strong more easily than the weak.

'Ten, twenty years from now, leaders of Western democracies will look the other way if we send tanks into Hungary of Czechoslovakia. They will pray for our success and as few casualties as possible, for their own political survival will be wholly dependent on our use of power. We must therefore concern ourselves with the business of peace, in which the West will prove itself a far more predictable partner than it would be in war. This was shown convincingly at Munich, and Iosif Vissarionovich never forgot the lesson. Certainly I have seen enough liberalization with my own eyes to know that there is no better way forward.

'Democracies have never understood that we have a strategy. They never had one, and when somebody does not know how to play chess and just "shuffles his galoshes" as we say, he always assumes his opponent is doing the same. They think Iosif Vissarionovich was a fool, Hitler a madman. Even if they could read what I am thinking now, and I mean the best of them, not $10,000-a-year riffraff in the State Department or those Yale spooks playing Cowboys and Injuns, they would never believe their eyes. They cannot comprehend that in war as in chess, the stronger your position the more productive the combinations you set up, until there is simply no room for failure left and your opponent surrenders.

'The most important thing, now that we are strong, is to feign weakness as we used to feign strength when we were weak. Peace will not come, and the West will never become our partner, unless we convince their electorates that this liberalization is not capricious like the others, but forced upon us by harsh reality: we are ready to be friends because they were such formidable enemies. And for this, as for everything else, we will need a new kind of media to influence their media, a new kind of public opinion to affect their public opinion. I accept your recommendation, comrades. I mean gentlemen.'

This, then, was the real question before Gorbachev: Was his mentor right?

Mrs Dejevsky's Profession

To understand how the West's media refracted the message of their suddenly 'free' Soviet counterpart, let us sample *The Times* mainstream, in contrast to the sparks of op-ed dissent already observed. As the dissent originates in the first circle of Sovietology's inferno of delusion, so does the mainstream of news and commentary from Moscow represent its lower depths.

One of the most significant events of the past few years in the British media's coverage of Soviet affairs occurred on 22 June 1988 and ought to be remembered as Christopher Walker's confession. Walker had been *The Times*'s 'man in Moscow' since November 1985 and his op-ed farewell to the post was entitled 'Moscow from the inside'. He began by revealing, for the first time since November 1985, that the 'ratio of KGB operatives employed for every foreigner living in Moscow' is, 'astonishingly enough, 14 to one'. The subsequent 1200 words of Walker's article could only be described as a wholesale repudiation of everything he had reported on a daily basis from Moscow during the previous three years. If that article never appeared, Walker would stand in the dock of history where Walter Duranty and others now stand. By writing it, he cleared his conscience, without, of course, undoing the damage already done. 'It is a dangerous atmosphere', Walker quoted a Moscow-based diplomat saying of the Western response to the Soviet change of tactics, 'in which to conduct arms control negotiations with far-reaching implications'. The diplomat might have added that it was his interlocutor who had helped to create that atmosphere at *The Times*.

Letting the proverbial scales fall from one's eyes and developing an analytical view of totalitarian reality are different things. Yet if the reader once again ignores the misleading 'Communist' and 'Party' components of the following insight, he may bestow upon Christopher Walker an honorary membership, however belated, in the first circle:

> *glasnost* is a carefully controlled Communist Party weapon, the purpose of which is to direct the spotlight of openness only where it is required for party reasons, and to maintain all too familiar restrictions where it is not.

As of 22 June 1988, Walker still honestly laboured under the delusion that the Communist Party mattered, and whatever scales had fallen from his eyes he continued to perceive the KGB as the Party's property. Nonetheless he felt obliged to note that

> The changing face of the KGB, whose surveillance technology Western intelligence estimates to be 10 years ahead of its own, is often forgotten by those whose main images come from televised scenes of KGB thugs attacking demonstrators. The neanderthals, with their tartan-plaid scarves and leather coats, still exist, but behind the scenes more subtle minds are at work.

Timidly, the erstwhile Moscow correspondent and now an op-ed dissident went on to speculate on the sponsorship by the KGB of such 'purveyors of the new image of the Soviet Union' as the weekly *Moscow News*. But even in his dissidence, Christopher Walker remained an anti-communist. To suppose that the 'Communist Party', and not only *Moscow News*, could become a front would have required unlearning everything he had ever known about 'Communism'.

As noted, nothing in Walker's three years of Moscow reporting had so much as hinted at the existence of some larger analytical picture into which individual news items might have fitted. 'Gorbachev tries to rewrite theory of Marxism', Walker reported on 15 November 1986, retelling a *Pravda* article published the day before. But the call for 'deep changes' in the 'Marxist theory of class struggle' alerted him only because *Pravda* used the word 'compromise' to describe the 'deep changes': in reality, what the article, one of many at the time, should have suggested, was that the new Soviet oligarchy was beginning to air its well-laid plans for switching from an alliance with 'world proletariat' to an alliance with 'world bourgeoisie', and that the wave of articles treated this tactical innovation in Marxist terms. Yet an 'anti-communist' like Walker was incapable of looking beyond the terminology to the underlying reality: soon to be effectively disenfranchised, the Communist Party was gradually being prepared for the inevitable moment when its KGB masters would ditch its traditionally 'pro-communist' allies in Western democracies and launch a world NEP under which wealth and commerce, not poverty and ideology, will deliver Western Europe into Soviet hands.

But even this myopic glimpse of the official Soviet press was exceptional, crowded as it was by endless Walker stories with no underlying meaning at all: about crime ('Kremlin wrath descends on prostitutes'), sport ('Glasnost comes to Soviet football'), alcoholism ('Russians dry out the American way'), banking ('Don't leave Vladivostok without it, Ivan') and so on.[31] In hundreds of thousands of column inches the very 'new image of the Soviet Union', whose purveyor Walker would identify as the KGB only months later, was being created at his newspaper and throughout the media on both sides of the Atlantic: Russia under Gorbachev was a European country like any other, only more backward, groping westward, towards capitalism and democracy, through a maze of ideological contradictions.

Shortly after Walker became his newspaper's Moscow man, a successor waited in the wings. Mary Dejevsky's remarkable *Times* début was made in an op-ed article in August 1986, entitled 'Moscow's other troop movement'.[32] This referred to the withdrawal of Soviet troops from Mongolia and, *inter alia*, to the Mongolians' 'national identity and the cult of Genghis Khan' as well as 'the persisting Russian folk memory of the Mongol invasion as a terror which must never be repeated'. Breathless platitudinizing of this kind is common in women's magazines, of course, as contributors tackle weighty issues of state to give their readers the illusion, as it were, that the world is not all pudding recipes and divorce. But it is a mistake to assume that 'serious journalism' is not easily reconciled with that tradition: it was precisely by employing the history-in-a-nutshell technique of human-interest, metro-desk reportage that Walter Duranty made his career with *The New York Times* in Stalin's Russia.

If in the figure of Gorbachev Soviet totalitarianism found a new Stalin, in the figure of Mrs Dejevsky -- if the past five years are any indication -- it found a new Duranty. To be sure, Moscow reporting by the *Guardian*, to the Left of *The Times,* has not been any more incisive or accurate.[33] But the uniqueness of Duranty's contribution to Sovietology, like that of Sir Bernard Pares in its earliest days (*Moscow Admits a Critic* was, significantly, the title of Pares's famous book), lay in his avowedly 'conservative' credentials and in the laboriously centrist position of his 'newspaper of record'. While in the United States today the influence of *The New York Times* is incomparably greater, in Britain the centre role of *The Times* is identical to that of *The New York Times* in the 1930s, even as the magnitude of the 'restructuring' in Russia today is a match for what took place under Stalin. It is for this reason that, like Gorbachev's propagandists, I find in *The Times* the key to Britain's political consensus.

Characteristically, early attempts by *The Times* management to secure Mary Dejevsky permanent accreditation were rebuffed by the relevant Soviet authorities, as the humiliating words 'From A Correspondent, Moscow' replaced Christopher Walker's familiar byline.[34] The implications were clear: his replacement would prove too unmanageable, too brave, too dangerous. A glance at the trial stories filed by Dejevsky in a single month of 1987 showed what sort of menace to the Soviet regime *The Times* was about to unleash: 'Russia outraged by plight of homeless children', 'Kremlin gloom on Afghan conflict', 'The cheque book invades a mystified Russia', 'Red tape strangles Moscow's rush for computer literacy', 'Kremlin tackles ailing and corrupt health system', 'Mother Teresa charity nuns to work in the Soviet Union', among others.[35] It is remarkable that a news report filed by the newspaper's defence editor on 20 August 1987, in the middle of Dejevsky's fearless exposé of Russia's dark underside, struck a note so different it might have embarrassed a less trivial-minded foreign correspondent. 'West is warned of Russia's silent submarine' ran the headline, and Michael Evans reported that according to the latest edition of *Jane's Fighting Ships*,

> the Soviet Union had "an armlock on the rest of the world in this department of science".... Although the potential of the new quieter system, known as magnetohydrodynamic thrust, had been known for 25 years, the West had not developed a similar system. Modern Soviet submarines are already well advanced because they are built with double hulls made of titanium alloys...

It is pointless to go on. Evans's non-ideological reality, observed in an office cubicle in Wapping, and Dejevsky's Moscow, where 'communist ideology' plays the part of local colour, are different worlds. One sees Moscow overtaking Nato in yet another strategic direction. The other watches it weep over computer illiteracy, war veterans and homeless children. One is based in London and concerned with 'defence', although in theory it would be more sensible to report *Jane's* revelations from Moscow. The other is concerned with nothing at all and bears the title of 'Moscow correspondent', although in practice it ought to be possible to peruse *Pravda* in London, if necessary with the help of a dictionary.[36]

From everything said so far it must be clear that the 'Plenum week' of 30 September 1988 was an important showcase of Soviet politics. 'Mary Dejevsky on today's crucial plenum in Moscow' was unambiguous: 'Gorbachev's big gamble', read the op-ed page headline. But why a gamble?

> Three hundred members of the Soviet Central Committee summoned urgently to Moscow will today decide the fate of Mikhail Gorbachev's reform programme, possibly of Gorbachev himself.[37]

To suggest, after more than 70 years of oligarchic or dictatorial totalitarianism in Russia, that congresses, conferences, plenums and the like can 'decide the fate' of an oligarch, not to mention a dictator, is wilful ignorance of Durantian proportions. Indeed, Dejevsky's own lead strives to conceal some fundamental ambivalence: if all these people can be 'summoned' by Gorbachev, how can they possibly 'decide the fate' of anything, not to mention Gorbachev or his programme? That the CC CPSU is a rubber-stamp of the Politburo was, apparently, unknown to Dejevsky. Yet this news is decades old. That in September 1988 the Politburo itself was on its way to becoming a rubber-stamp, first *de facto* and then *de jure*, is the news she did not report then or since.

> While Soviet officials have sought to play down the meeting's significance...

Of course they have. Several hundred high party functionaries bundled into cars like so many clowns just because something needs to be rubber-stamped? Even Stalin never trampled party decorum quite so ruthlessly. But Dejevsky goes on:

> ...the tension on the face of Gennady Gerasimov, the usually genial foreign ministry spokesman, as he broke the news said much.

Gerasimov need not have worried, for this is what was on Dejevsky's mind:

> The Olympic Games, in which the Soviet team has had great successes, are reaching their climax. The weekend mood could have been one of relaxed triumph. It might still be. Gorbachev has shown himself a master of the pre-emptive strike.

In other words, Gorbachev is in danger from party officials (whom he had just had bundled into cars like clowns and dragged to Moscow?), but as so often in the past he 'might still' save himself (and the ebullient mood of Soviet sports fans).

> It may be that his patience has finally snapped, or that he now senses growing popular support for faster and more far-reaching change than the Communist Party apparatus will permit...

Where could that powerful 'popular' support be lodged, a *Times* reader might have wondered. In the Moscow metro? In pubs? Among homeless children? Apparently not:

> Might he use the meeting to issue a dramatic challenge to the Central Committee to support him or remove him?

So Gorbachev 'summoned' them to issue a 'dramatic challenge' roughly along these lines: Sack me or let me keep my job, I can't stand the suspense any longer!

> Such high-risk tactics are not alien to Gorbachev. The special party conference last June... was widely interpreted as an attempt by Gorbachev to demonstrate the necessity of change and the support for it from rank and file Communists.

Is this, then, where that powerful 'popular' support lies? In 'rank and file Communists'? Yet read the next sentence:

> Some saw it as an attempt to bypass the Central Committee altogether.

In other words, the year before, in June 1987, 'some' realised that the days of the CC CPSU, *de jure* and not only *de facto*, were numbered. Who knows, 'some' others probably suspected that the Politburo was not far behind, or that the 'C' in 'CPSU' would one day stand for 'Capitalist', 'Clean', or 'Cuddly'. But Dejevsky was not among them as, fifteen months later, she failed to understand that the secret-police apparatus then in power could 'bypass' the Central Committee *de facto* as easily as the earlier Soviet oligarchies had bypassed it. The news in June 1987 was that it had been bypassed *de jure*, even as in September 1988 the news was that it had been bypassed in such a way as to inflict maximum humiliation upon its members.

'Gorbachev's majority in the Politburo', Dejevsky concluded her prognostication, 'slender when he took over, looks scarcely more secure today'. The *Times* reader could never have known that neither the 'majority' of Dejevsky's conjecture nor the Politburo as a whole was where power lay that September, and consequently Dejevsky's 'big gamble' could never have been seen for what it was.

But lest it be thought that my portrayal of Dejevsky as the new Duranty is a personal vendetta, it should be mentioned that subsequent *Times* coverage of the 'Plenum week' was carried out by the anonymous 'Correspondent, Moscow' who remained true to the Dejevsky tradition of passive replication of Soviet press releases only occasionally enlivened by wild speculation and the odd human-interest touch. It was difficult to describe that week of reporting from Moscow as anything but tragicomic. In fact, so well does the epithet apply to the inner reaches of the Sovietological inferno that the American left-wing satirical monthly *SPY* recently featured a sample of the agglomerated absurdity entitled 'A Kopeck for His Thoughts'. The emphasis is *SPY*'s and the quotations below, from *Foreign Affairs, Time, The Sunday Telegraph, The Christian Science Monitor, U.S. News & World Report,* again *The Christian Science Monitor, The Washington Post, The New York Times, Los Angeles Times,* again *The New York Times*, and *San Francisco Chronicle* respectively, are only a few of those held up to ridicule in the magazine's survey:

> "The bitter and frustrating experience of the Russians for the last decade in Afghanistan was **doubtless in Gorbachev's mind** at the Communist Party Congress."
>
> "Soviet problems with ethnic unrest will **doubtless be very much on Gorbachev's mind** this week."
>
> "Uppermost **in Mr. Gorbachev's mind was clearly** Nikita Khrushchev's coup of June 1957."
>
> "The cost of defense has **long been on Mr. Gorbachev's mind**."
>
> "[The Ukraine's] economic importance **clearly preys on Mikhail**

Gorbachev's mind."
"The hulking Soviet economy, groping towards modernity, is **never far from Gorbachev's mind.**"
"Gorbachev seems **confused, and often angered**, by the rise of nationalism under his watch."
"Gorbachev has been enormously **frustrated** by the Nagorno-Karabakh dispute."
"Gorbachev may be **confused** but does not appear worried."
"According to an elected official who has seen him recently, 'Gorbachev is **upset, unstable, unlike himself** of a year ago.'"
"For years Mikhail Gorbachev was **deeply worried** about the terrible shape of the Soviet economy. And he still is."[38]

In short, Andropov's advisers were right when they forecasted that the mainstream Western media would not penetrate the facade of *glasnost*. The problem with Mrs Dejevsky is her profession. As her predecessor at *The Times,* Christopher Walker, would now concede, no Moscow correspondent has ever been anything other than a fool or a knave, and when he acts as a Sovietologist the combination of these qualities launches a shameless lie for which posterity will hold him responsible, as it now holds Walter Duranty. As far as Soviet propagandists are concerned, however, posterity is not their department.

The Shape of Things to Come

'As I write, highly civilised human beings are flying overhead, trying to kill me', Orwell began *The Lion and the Unicorn.* The present is no less momentous.

It is naive to assume that the lower depths of the Sovietological inferno -- that is, of Western ignorance and ineptitude in the study of totalitarianism -- are where they have always been politically. The new strategy of totalitarianism has made havoc of the political spectrum in Western democracies, and the Right today is scarcely less inclined to self-deception than the Left. 'Labour Party politics had become a variant of Conservatism', Orwell remarked in the same essay, written when Munich was still fresh in his memory. In the winter of 1940, this obituary of the political spectrum -- and consequently of democratic debate -- was a prophetic paradox. In the winter of 1990, the prophecy is fulfilled so completely that free human beings will probably never again be bombed from the air. The way from the present to the future is a way of peace.

Like Caesar or Napoleon, Hitler pursued his aim of world conquest extensively, seeking to add territory after territory to his possessions. Despite the presence of a clear and present danger, democracies failed to prepare for war, and those within Nazi Germany's reach collapsed when it came. Had Hitler persisted in the more subtle strategy of Munich, it is likely that Churchill would have remained 'exiled from power, largely distrusted by both major parties, thought to lack judgement and stability' (*Encyclopedia Britannica,* 1973), while Hitler would have dominated the world.

Building on the subtler components of strategies conceived by Stalin, today's Soviet oligarchs and tomorrow's dictators are developing a new, 'Munich' approach to world conquest: *intensive*, rather than *extensive*.[39] Their aim is a gradual, controlled integration of totalitarianism into Western democracies, whereby science and technology, historically a bulwark of the West's power and autarchy, will pass into their hands in exchange for promised peace and stability. In the process, a Eurasian 'New Economic Policy' -- complete with a Europe 'unified' of its own accord, as well as robust capitalism and equally robust disarmament -- will conceal the erosion of individual liberties and the passing of all authority to the new Eurasia's sole military superpower, its fist of nuclear blackmail gloved by the Urals.

The West's ideologically-minded Sovietologists, who cannot see totalitarianism for the communists, have never understood the NEP for the great experiment it was. Yet, however limited, capitalism coexisted with totalitarianism even under Stalin and Hitler, and there is no historical evidence to show that, should this be needed by totalitarian oligarchs for their strategy to succeed, capitalism or even 'democracy' cannot flourish in the new Eurasia in the absence of Western political freedoms for as long as it suits Moscow. Until when? Until such time as the industrial potential of the new Eurasia is mobilised in the service of future expansion, to the American continent, China, and in the turbulent Muslim world. Even an eyewitness of Pol Pot's crimes against humanity could never conceive of the hell-on-earth that a mobilising totalitarianism, limited by nothing from without, will establish on the stretch of territory from Ireland to Japan.

Above, 'democracy' is in inverted commas because the West's ideologically-minded Sovietologists have never understood its realities. If one calls its genuine counterpart 'Western democracy', one can confidently say that it is an achievement greater than all the other achievements of civilisation combined, for without it, as this century has shown, all these achievements become mere tools of tyranny. Yet one can say with equal confidence that the growing pains of 'Soviet democracy' are a process by which democracy itself is to become just another of these tools. As for capitalism, there, comparatively speaking, the counterfeit and the real are a hair's breadth apart to begin with, because men's communal need to 'buy, sell and otherwise contract with one another', in Hobbes's phrase, is so much stronger than their need of intellectual or spiritual sovereignty, or dissent, by which individual liberty may be measured.

Freedom is the exercise of freedom. It is not a matter of choice but of meaningful choice, and outside the context of power its precious meaning is an abstraction. Contestants on a television game show who 'choose' answers, 'find' treasure or 'pick' their dates are deceiving the audience, often by mutual consent, into a simulacrum of genuine action. They have neither the means nor the desire to challenge the rules of the game, which is recognised as such by the audience. By contrast, in Western democracies the electoral process takes place against the background of national sovereignty guaranteed by the force of arms and of civil order ensured by customs and traditions, within a pluralist society composed of a myriad special interests, many of which have something to gain from the genuineness of the process and something to lose from the narrowing of political choice. Nonetheless, democracy's detractors, who are found in every social stratum, often dismiss the election of 'politicians' as a game.

If Western democracy is so widely perceived as a closed system of monopoly political interest, what can be said of the Soviet simulacrum? If 'politicians' like Havel or Walesa, not to mention Landsbergis or Yeltsin, lack so much as a meaningful deterrent against intimidation from without, what hope have they or their 'constituents' for meaningful choice within? For, in a global perspective, even Western nuclear powers retain their freedom only insofar as they can demonstrably retain their sovereignty in opposition to Soviet military power, whose global strategic projection already translates into political influence in Western democracies. To ignore the continuing growth of that influence, whatever illusory retreats or momentary detours Soviet totalitarianism may devise along the way, is to lead what remains of this free world into eternal slavery.

This is why, today, in the depths of Sovietology's inferno, E. H. Carrs and Beatrice Webbs, with their New Statesmen and Nations, are not Seweryn Bialers and Archie Browns with their Guardians and Columbia Journalism Reviews. Today's deceivers and self-deceivers are our Walter Laqueurs and Robert Conquests, our Telegraphs and Wall Street Journals, those 'anti-communists' of yesteryear who have welcomed the 'new openness' of a 'restructuring' totalitarianism with a triumphal arch of ignorance worthy of Chamberlain.

'True', Laqueur concedes in the concluding chapter of his latest book, 'the Soviet Union has become a superpower'. 'This', he goes on to say, 'has brought pride to some but not greater happiness'.[40] What one sees at the very bottom of Sovietology's inferno today, however unrecognisable its political disposition, is what has lain there since 1917: pathetic reluctance of the West to comprehend that the pursuit of happiness is not on totalitarianism's agenda. It is accurate enough to say that the Right in Western democracies, newly blinded by Soviet capitalism and 'democracy', is as disinclined to look beyond the fictions in the 1990s as the Left was in the 1930s. It is more accurate to say that if, as Orwell noted, in the Nazi peace of the 1930s Labour thinking was a variant of Conservatism, it is 'anti-communism' in the Soviet peace of the 1990s that sustains the identically bipartisan consensus.

In the autumn of 1987 *The Times* ran a 'series on the Russian Revolution', with Connor Cruise O'Brien among the contributors 'on the Left' and Robert Conquest among those 'on the Right'. Needless to say, O'Brien's contribution included traditional admissions like 'Of course it wasn't all sweetness and light' (in Stalin's Russia) and equally traditional insistence that '"The Great Patriotic War" was not an empty phrase' (of Stalin's). But consider this insight. 'Up to 1943', writes O'Brien,

> it was a common assumption in 'informed circles' in the West that the Soviet Union was about to break up. What is perhaps surprising is that this belief should still be around. That the polity which survived invasion by the Wehrmacht can be brought to dissolution by such gimmicks as 'smuggling copies of the Koran into Central Asia' is an article of faith among large numbers of American conservatives.[41]

By contrast, Conquest's article contained not a single insight of comparable value. It contained traditional disdain for the fellow-travelling past of 'American liberalism' and 'British socialism', and equally traditional debunking of the 'myths of Marxism' (which, as the author admits, 'flourish today' only among 'half-educated army officers in Ethiopia' and 'quarter-educated English lecturers in California'). But the moral, as it were, is this:

> It is true that the doctrines of the Revolution have ostentatiously failed to produce a superior or even a tolerable society; indeed that the whole system is, economically and otherwise, barely viable. In the long run, something has to give. But dogma is deep-rooted; basic motivations do not change easily; and the system has enormous momentum and inertia.

These, I maintain, are the lowest depths of Sovietology's inferno. Seven decades after the fact, and two decades after his own *Great Terror,* Conquest in 1987 -- like Laqueur still later, in 1990 -- discovers that no 'tolerable society' has ever existed under totalitarianism (and that, presumably, if it had then totalitarianism would not have been such a bad thing after all). As if this is not enough, he goes on -- living up to O'Brien's contemptuous image of blithe 'conservatives' -- to argue that 'the whole system' is 'barely viable'. Let us eat, drink and be merry.

For tomorrow never comes to those who live by hindsight. Of course Conquest is only too delighted to throw in some caveats: 'We should not confuse', he advises, 'words with deeds' even while we 'welcome fundamental change as, and to the degree to which, it occurs' in Russia. But his foundational assumption is that Soviet totalitarianism -- 'the polity which survived invasion by the Wehrmacht' in O'Brien's mild phrase, the 'polity' whose strategic infrastructure has achieved superiority over the West, the 'polity' that now rules the oceans and commands the frontiers of space -- is... a baby. Yes, a baby, and Conquest concludes his article as follows:

> We do not say, when we welcome a baby's first tottering step, that it need do no more. We encourage it to take another. And another.[42]

Opposing the consensus, as my friend Barbara Amiel, a 'Conservative' *Times* journalist whose career has survived her steadfast refusal to mouth party-political slogans, recently wrote, does not prove that one is on the side of truth. Yet here Miss Amiel would have to agree that a scholar who treats the object of his scholarship in terms so patently infantile is, irrespective of his party-political affiliation, a baby.

Opposing the consensus does not, in and of itself, prove that one is on the side of truth. Yet if a mass fiction, such as the 'collapse of communism', has a clearly traceable party-political motivation behind it, one's duty is to look beyond the fiction no matter how unpleasant what one may see. The motivation, in this case, is hard to miss: by hailing the Gorbachev 'revolution' in Russia and Eastern Europe, the Right in Western democracies has stolen the peace march on the Left and can now offer the electorate a disarmament dividend, in the past a traditional Labour dream in Britain, traditionally shattered at election time by the man-in-the-street awareness of Soviet reality.

Thus when the new regime established by the secret-police apparatus unveiled the Trojan horse of *perestroika* in Moscow it provided Western politicians with the elements of a new electoral consensus which they badly needed to increase their chances of staying in power. If totalitarianism 'restructured' itself to appear less menacing, democracies could claim victory and respond by slashing their defence budgets. In Britain this meant that a bigger boon than all previous electoral bribes of 'privatisation' was in the offing, a more spectacular initiative than all previous machinations of 'European Community leadership' was under way. All that was lacking was the myth that it had been the earlier show of strategic resolve by the West which had weakened Soviet totalitarianism to the point of collapse and forced it onto the path of introspection and change.

Such, then, was the inducing motivation behind Western foreign-policy decisions and Soviet propaganda efforts to justify them by publicizing, 'under *glasnost*', misleading part-truths rather than straightforward lies. Again, this innovation was foreseen by Orwell who wrote at the beginning of the last war that the 'threatening tone' of enemy propaganda was a psychological mistake: England's surrender, he warned, 'could happen most easily when the war seemed to be going well rather than badly'. Thus, for the first time since the break-up of the West's alliance with Stalin against Hitler, Soviet totalitarianism and Western democracy had a common political objective: to prove that the former was as militarily weak as the latter was strong.

If the motive had been there all along, traditionally confined to the Left of the political spectrum, it was Afghanistan that presented the Right with the opportunity. The Soviet invasion in 1979 had ended the earlier spring of détente, giving the West fresh resolve to resist Soviet expansionism and new governments believed capable of the task. In reality, by seizing control of the strategically valuable 12 percent of Afghan territory and fortifying it with some 170 military bases, including 15 airfields, the Soviet commander, General Valentin Varennikov, was able to turn the theatre of war into political theatre: CIA-supported mujahideen had a free run outside his 'Fortress Afghanistan' for the Western media to applaud their successes. By 1988, when the Soviet pullout began, the Soviet and Western press alike could describe Varennikov's brilliant victory as an ignominious failure without any reference to the fact that Afghanistan had been conquered.

The Soviet 'defeat' in Afghanistan, as covered in the Soviet press even before the official launch of *glasnost*, was the blueprint which the new Soviet oligarchy would use in restructuring the set of permissions and prohibitions extending to Soviet journalists, politicians, spokesmen and anyone with any potential for affecting Western public opinion. The spotlight of anguished inquiry could now be turned on the seamy underside of Soviet life, something that most of the regime's internal critics ('dissidents' like Andrei Sakharov) had not dreamed possible and something its critics abroad ('anti-communists' like Robert Conquest) had enjoyed doing for decades: from Stalin's crimes to food shortages, from latent nationalism to cultural stagnation, nothing seemed forbidden. Few in Russia perceived, to quote a recent editorial in one *samizdat* journal, that totalitarianism can 'take any idea and, so long as it glides past its vital organs, invert, assimilate and turn that idea to its own advantage'.[43] Few in the West perceived that freedom of expression, unless it is a democratically enforced absolute, is just such an idea.

Thus poor old communism, once convenient as an ideology, could be replaced by the new totalitarian oligarchy at the expense of the poor old Communist Party with such 'Western-style' values as liberty, prosperity, property. So long as they are embraced only verbally, all such universals glide past the vital organs of totalitarianism and, unchallenged in the West, only strengthen the oligarchy's stranglehold on its subjects.

After Afghanistan came Eastern Europe. Here these new 'ideas' and new 'freedoms' -- limited, as ever before, by Soviet military might, though no longer poised menacingly over the threshold --

could be tested with impunity. Indeed, so long as the new democracies have no meaningful deterrent against the *possibility* of Soviet clampdown, as in Czechoslovakia in 1948 or 1968, their civic development is as conditional as it is in the Baltic republics, or wherever else the axe may suddenly fall as it did in Tiananmen Square. Yet part-truths like the Czech government's recent revelation that it had come to power as the result of a KGB operation 'gone wrong'[44] have successfully blinded Western electorates to the truth that Eastern Europe has not been set free. It has been traded, a chess piece in the new game of superdétente, for unlimited access to Western science and technology.

And here the fear of fear with which I began comes full circle. Even those who concede that the KGB, and not the tooth fairy, has 'opened up' Russia and 'liberated' Eastern Europe fail to recognise in science and technology the very hangman's rope which Lenin promised the West would sell. The obstacle in the path of recognition is, once again, 'Soviet economic collapse', which the Soviet media -- and, following or anticipating them, the West's Moscow correspondents and academic Sovietologists -- have been permitted, indeed encouraged, to uncover along with other bleeding sores of the body politic. For if the Soviet system is collapsing, science and technology will not save it, and Western businessmen can once again, in Orwell's words of 1940, 'tumble over one another' in their eagerness to sell totalitarianism the best rope money can buy. As Gorbachev's mentor Andropov, speaking of the secret-police apparatus he had headed before the coup which brought him to power said publicly: 'If our [KGB] emblem were being designed today one would boldly add a symbol of modern electronics alongside the sword and shield'.[45]

The bitter truth before us, then, is that the 'free' Soviet press has been allowed to focus on internal failure because this justifies the new course of superdétente. It has done a good job not because the KGB managed the deception from one day to the next, but because the Soviet civilian economy has been in a state of collapse since 1917, just as the Soviet strategic infrastructure has prospered since 1917 and, since 1963, achieved nuclear parity with and then superiority over its Nato adversary. The current transfer of science and technology, especially in its prospective dimensions in the coming days of the pan-Eurasian NEP when totalitarianism puts on a capitalist face, will render that superiority irreversible, and the lines separating Eastern and Western Europe will finally become as meaningless as constitutional guarantees or parliamentary proceedings in a world of naked and irrefutable force.[46]

The importance of the Fourth Estate has been increasing in Western democracies in proportion to the faltering of debate between the major political parties. To Karl Kraus's vicious certainty, 'Politicians tell lies to journalists and then believe what they read', in the twilight of this totalitarian century has been added another: Journalists tell lies to politicians and then believe what they hear. To what extent will the free press of a disarming Western Europe mirror the delusions, whether spontaneous or induced, of its counterpart in the unarmed Central Europe? How closely will it replicate the deceptions, whether conscious or unconscious, of the unfree Soviet press when the simulacrum of capitalism and 'democracy' becomes a pan-Eurasian reality? On the answer to these questions depends the success of *perestroika*, by which I mean the successful projection of Soviet totalitarianism's military and political influence beyond the closed world on whose frontiers the Berlin Wall once stood.

A spectre is haunting Europe. It is the spectre of anti-communism. 'The only people who are *never* converted to spiritualism are conjurers', joked Orwell, and as I take my leave I ask the ladies and gentlemen of the press for whom this essay was written to think why that spectre is any more real, or ultimately more benign, than the one unleashed upon them by totalitarian conjurers earlier in the century.

1 January 1991 Cambridge.

Notes

1. 'If you are caught committing any of these crimes on a small scale, you are punished and disgraced; they call it sacrilege, kidnapping, burglary, theft and brigandage. But if, besides taking their property, you turn all your countrymen into slaves, you will hear no more of these ugly words; your countrymen themselves will call you the happiest of men and bless your name.' Only in the twentieth century can Plato's paradox be said to have come alive in its totalitarian dimensions.

2. The influence of *The New York Times* as America's only general-interest national daily source of serious news and opinion may well be greater, and not necessarily more benign, than that of the Communist Party's *Pravda* in Russia.

3. Carl von Clausewitz, *On War,* ed. Anatol Rapaport (Harmondsworth, Middlesex: Penguin Books, 1968).

4. Anatoly Golitsyn, *New Lies for Old* (London: Bodley Head, 1984).

5. In *Totalitarianism at the Crossroads,* ed. Ellen Frankel Paul (New Brunswick, USA, and London: Transaction Books, 1990), pp. 97-142.

6. Viktor Suvorov, *Icebreaker* (London: Hamish Hamilton, 1990). 'Allbecrushing intellect', The Times, 5 May 1990.

7. Roger Scruton, 'The evil that is done by diplomatic lies', *Sunday Telegraph,* 22 April 1990.

8. *Letters to the Editor, The Times, 25 October 1990.* A book-length presentation of Crozier's thesis, in which facts suppressed or ignored by the consensus are to be found side by side with ideologically-motivated suppositions and 'anti-communist' fictions, is *The Gorbachev Phenomenon* (London: The Claridge Press, 1988).

9. 'Not without honour', leading article, *The Times,* 16 October 1990.

10 As this essay went to press, reachers of the *Telegraph* were treated to a glowing profile of 'Miss KGB' by the newspaper's Moscow correspondent, while Moscow pulled its subsidy from the Communist *Morning Star* in Britain, dooming it to eventual bankruptcy. It is difficult to think of two media events that

better capture the contradictions of the 'political spectrum' in our time.

11. 'Prize piety', leading article, *The Times*, 14 October 1987.

12. 'The press and its politics', *The Sunday Times*, 23 August 1987.

13. 8 October 1987.

14. 1 March 1988.

15. 6 May 1989.

16. Gerald Frost, 'The sub-zero option that faces Europe', *The Times*, 20 August 1987.

17. 'Scepticism about "glasnost"', leading article, *The Independent*, 4 November 1987.

18. *The National Interest*, Autumn 1988, p.99.

19. Peter Stothard, 'Life and whole of the party', *The Times*, 20 September 1988.

20. David Owen, 'Moscow's nuclear endgame', *The Times*, 29 January 1988.

21. Made in February 1989, first British broadcast in May 1989.

22. Alun Chalfont, 'Can Thatcher rally Europe?', *The Times*, 19 February 1988.

23. For more on the effects of political thinking within the consensus, see Andrei Navrozov, 'Why I am Not a Conservative', *The Salisbury Review*, September 1990.

24. 'Arkansas Town Split', *New York Tribune*, 8 December 1987.

25. Ronald Reagan, *An American Life* (London: Hutchinson, 1990), p. 696.

26. On the INF treaty's inexhaustible absurdities, see *The Treaty on Intermediate-range Nuclear Weapons: Does It Decrease or Increase the Danger of Nuclear War?*, memorandum of 25 January 1988 to members of the Senate Foreign Relations Committee from Senator Jesse Helms. The content of this 180-page published document has never been mentioned in any British newspaper.

27. *The Times*, 5 September 1988. *The New York Times*, 5 September 1988.

28. *U.S. News & World Report*, 24 October 1988, p.17.

29. Sadly for his Western admirers, even unprecedented dictatorial powers cannot guarantee political longevity in Gorbachev's case. He is a dictator by the grace of the secret-police apparatus: what it giveth, it can also take away. The issue here is not Gorbachev's 'lib-

eralism', of course, since if the KGB deems it expedient to stop or turn back the clock of reform he will have no alternative but to do its bidding, convincingly and with enthusiasm. But should the KGB find Gorbachev outmoded or ineffective, it has at its disposal plenty of fiery 'liberals' ready to step into the dictator's role and will replace its super-Stalin as easily as Stalin used to replace his secret-police chiefs.

30. It is noteworthy that it was in July 1990 that the old-fashioned law against 'Anti-Soviet Agitation and Propaganda', under which old-fashioned dissidents used to be suppressed, gave way to the squeaky-clean new law 'On the Protection of Honour and Dignity of the President' which carries sentences of three years' imprisonment for private expressions of criticism directed at Gorbachev personally. The old-fashioned dissident Valeriya Novodvorskaya was the first to be arrested under the squeaky-clean new law.

31. Titles of stories by Christopher Walker, *The Times*, 17 November 1986, 21 September 1987, 2 February 1988 and 3 March 1988.

32. *The Times*, 4 August 1986.

33. In a 1986 book review I described Martin Walker's *The Waking Giant* as 'a chatty, urbane paean to the gentrification of totalitarianism by *The Guardian*'s man in Moscow' ('Doubtful art of Kremlinology', *The Times*, 13 November 1986). Two omnipresent beadles of the *Guardian* school of Sovietology provide nightly entertainment on BBC news broadcasts under the Dickensian, or Dostoyevskian, names of Peter 'Frank' and Alex 'Pravda'.

34. Assuming perhaps that 'the Kremlin authorities' had somehow misunderstood its way of playing hardball, *The Times* in a leader on Mrs Dejevsky's accreditation difficulties published after many months of behind-the-scenes pleading ('Glasnost and The Times', 30 March 1989) stressed that her alleged 'language skills and deep knowledge of the Soviet system make her a journalist whom the Kremlin authorities would prefer to keep out of the country'.

35. Mary Dejevsky's stories, *The Times*, 13, 18, 20, 21, 24 and 25 August 1987.

36. I have yet to meet a Western academic specialist in Soviet studies, not to mention a Moscow correspondent of a Western newspaper, who speaks 'fluent' Russian. Yet the very standard of 'fluency' is inadequate when what one is called upon to interpret is not a

menu touristique but a closed society whose associations with pre-1917 Russia and its language are more often than not deliberately falsified. In this connection, I can recall nothing more hilarious than the dead-pan bluff ('Between the party lines', *The Daily Telegraph,* 16 January 1989) of Xan Smiley, one of the *Telegraph*'s Soviet experts (especially now that Rhodesia, his previous field of expertise, has ceased to exist, thanks in part to incisive reporting on the subject of 'the black man' in Africa). 'The dailies are written two days ahead, sanitised by the editors', ran Smiley's expose of Soviet media. 'I can barely recall seeing a misprint in two years.' With all due respect, no Soviet expert I have ever come across, and certainly not Smiley, could identify a misprint in a Russian-language newspaper even if half the words in it were spelt backwards.

37. *The Times*, 30 September 1988.

38. *SPY*, June 1990, page 44.

39. The first use of these terms to distinguish between pre- and post-Brezhnev strategic *modus operandi* was made by Lev Navrozov in the founding statement of the Center for the Survival of Western Democracies, a private non-profit research group he has directed since 1978.

40. Walter Laqueur, *Stalin: The Glasnost Revelations* (London: Unwin Heimann, 1990) p. 278.

41. 'A new shade of red across the map', *The Times*, 30 October 1987.

42. 'Lenin's legacy: a world of danger', *The Times*, 27 October 1987. In this connection, see my reviews of Conquest's *Stalin and the Kirov Murder* ('Big brother watching', *The Times*, 4 May 1989) and *The Great Terror: A Reassessment* ('No intellectual backbone', *The Spectator*, 1 September 1990), which did not fail to draw an angered private response from the author's fellow 'anti-communists' on both sides of the Atlantic as I am certain my review of Laqueur will do.

43. Uchreditel'noye sobraniye [Constituent Assembly], 30 October 1989. The periodical is produced on a photocopying machine.

44. The well-publicized part-truths include incontrovertible evidence that the KGB masterminded at least some, if not all, of the 'revolutions' in Eastern Europe. For Czechoslovakia, see 'Prague revolution "engineered by the secret police"', *The Times,* 30 May 1990. The author, John Simpson, Foreign Affairs Editor of the BBC, timed the article to correspond with

the airing on BBC2 of the documentary he had scripted, *Czech-Mate*. Information on which both the documentary and the article were based had been made available to the BBC by the Czech 'parliamentary commission' of inquiry eager to demonstrate that 'Mr Havel and the Civic Forum were swept into government by immense public enthusiasm, the beneficiaries of an unlikely plot by their worst enemies', the KGB. For a similar 'all's well that ends well' scenario in East Germany, see 'Plots and conspiricies', *The Daily Telegraph*, 6 November 1990, reviewing Channel 4's documentary *And the Walls Came Tumbling Down*. In Poland no radical subversion of the old Brezhnevite leadership was necessary, as Walesa's Solidarity had already done the KGB's work of ushering in 'Polish democracy'.

45. Yuri Andropov, Izbranyye rechi i stat'i [Selected Speeches and Articles] (Moscow: Politizdat, 1979), p.124.

46. An abridged version of this section appeared in *The Daily Telegraph* under the title 'The false new freedoms' on 29 November 1990.